SWITZERLAND - A MODEL OF FEDERAL DEMOCRACY

Richard Wildblood

Quacks Books
York

Also by Richard Wildblood:
What Makes Switzerland Tick?
and
What Makes Switzerland Unique?

© Richard Wildblood 1993
All rights reserved by copyright owner

ISBN 0 948333 13 8

First published in 1993
by
Quacks Books
Petergate, York, YO1 2HT
Tel: 0904 625148
Fax: 0904 610649

British Library Cataloguing in Publication Data
Wildblood, Richard
Switzerland - A Model of Federal Democracy

Printed in 11/12 point Baskerville typeface
by Quacks the Booklet Printers
7 Grape Lane, Petergate,
York, YO1 2HU
Tel: 0904 635967

CONTENTS

Page

Introduction	1
The Swiss Pattern of Federalism	2
Comments on Swiss Federalism	4
The Swiss Pattern of Political Organisation	5
Comments on Swiss Political Organisation	7
The Swiss Pattern of Legislative Procedure	8
Characteristics of Swiss Legislative Procedure	10
The Swiss Pattern of Political Representation	11
Comments on the Swiss Pattern of Political Representation	13
The Swiss Pattern of Direct Democracy	14
Distinctive Features of the Swiss Political System	15
Subsidiarity	15
The Militia-system	15
The Sovereignty of the People	16
The Cult of Achieving Consensus	17
The Cult of Equity	18
Political Attributes of the Swiss People	20

INTRODUCTION

I think today it can be fairly claimed that Switzerland has one of the most democratic political structures of any country in the world. This development did not materialize overnight, but is the product of a long period of political experimentation and gradual progression.

The first democratic concepts of political organisation were brought to that part of central Europe which we now call Switzerland by a Germanic tribe called the Alemanni, when they invaded the northern parts of the Roman Empire in the year 260 AD. The early rudimentary democratic perceptions which they brought with them, such as the practice of community decision-making being made at public meetings by all the warriors of the tribe, or a self-elected legal system, were eclipsed for a time when the Franks, another Germanic tribe, in their turn invaded Switzerland and brought with them the feudal system, but they never fully died out. They revived at the end of the Middle Ages and reappeared at the creation of the Old Swiss Confederation in 1291 AD, when men from the cantons of Uri, Schwyz and Unterwalden swore an oath of allegiance to each other on the shores of Lake Lucerne.

Other Swiss cantons quickly joined the three founder members and over the years democracy slowly developed in their territories. In 1848 the desire for closer co-operation prompted them to create a new Swiss Confederation with a democratic federal constitution. This constitution was revised in 1874, but despite minor amendments, it has remained much the same since that date.

It is because of her long democratic tradition and development, resulting in this mature Swiss federal political structure, and the responsible political attitudes developed by the operators of that political system, namely the Swiss people themselves, that Switzerland's political experience of federal democracy may be presented as a pattern to the outside world. This short booklet is an attempt to do just that.

THE SWISS PATTERN OF FEDERALISM

Switzerland is a federation of twenty-six states called cantons (six of which are regarded as half cantons) with a national Federal authority acting as an umbrella organisation over the whole. The cantons are divided up into around 3,060 smaller political units called communes.

These Swiss cantons are not merely administrative areas of a centralized state, but rather independent small states; they have their own constitutions, create their own authorities, elect their own governments, parliaments and administrative bodies. They also have their own law-courts and levy their own taxes. The national Federal Law only prescribes certain basic requirements for the cantons. The Federal State authority cannot impose a governor on a canton; it may only intervene in a canton if the cantonal government requests it to do so to restore law and order, or if cantonal government has completely broken down.

It is the aim of federalism in Switzerland to leave as much decision making as possible to the cantons. Over a period of time since 1848, a division of competences has had to be worked out between the Federal State and the cantons. In the drawing up of the Federal Constitution in 1848, only those tasks were deputed to the Federal State which were of common interest to all the cantons, or which the Federal State would be better able to carry out than the cantons themselves, and they were clearly laid down and defined. To these belong the preservation of peace, both external and internal, foreign affairs, the protection of the rights of Swiss citizens and cantons, the safeguarding of cantonal institutions, the minting of money, the post and telegraph services, explosives, railways, shipping, air-transport, customs dues, certain military organisation, the control of weights and measures and the promotion of the economic well-being of the Swiss State, among others. The Federal State authorities also supervise the Swiss National Bank, which is an independent institution.

All those competencies which are not specifically assigned to the Federal State in the Swiss Federal Constitution are the concern of the cantons. Certain of these are deputed by the cantons to the communes. The commune, however, is not merely the lowest organ of state administration; the communes also enjoy a certain amount of autonomy, in that they have their own constitutions, governments and administrations and they also levy their own taxes. The communes are, however, subject to cantonal law.

Comments on Swiss Federalism

a. Although at the creation of the new Swiss Confederation in 1848 the cantons reluctantly surrendered a minimum of autonomy to the new overall Federal State authority, they still retained a very large part of their sovereignty. Moreover, in that the cantons collectively have powers to demand a revision of the Federal Constitution by means of a referendum of people and cantons, they have the means to restrict the power of Federal authority.

b. In a federal democratic organisation the criterion is not so much whether the overall political authority or the component parts are predominantly autonomous, but whether ultimate political sovereignty is vested in the people, where in a democracy political power truly belongs.

THE SWISS PATTERN OF POLITICAL ORGANISATION

In the Swiss Federal Constitution political authority at national level is divided between three political agencies, namely the Legislature (Parliament), the Executive (Government) and the Judiciary (Federal Supreme Court).

The Legislature or Federal Parliament, consists of two chambers which are elected democratically by the Swiss people, namely the National Council representing the people and the States Council representing the cantons.

The National Council is composed of 200 deputies and is elected mainly by the proportional representation voting-system, whereas the States Council has 46 members who are chosen mainly by the majority voting-system. In the States Council each full canton has two members and each half canton one representative irrespective of the size of the canton. Elections to both houses are held every four years.

The two chambers are of equal standing and all legislation must be passed by both, in identical form, to become law. The principal tasks assigned to the Federal Parliament are to legislate, authorize the national budget and accept the Federal accounts for the past year, exercise supervision over the Federal Administration and, most important, meet together as the Federal Assembly and elect both the Federal Council (Executive) and the Federal Supreme Court (Judiciary), namely the judges who make up that court. All Swiss members of Parliament, both Federal, cantonal and communal are part-time, voluntary or semi-voluntary representatives.

The Federal Council is composed of seven members drawn from the four largest political parties in accordance with what is known as the 'Magic Formula'; that is two members are elected from the Swiss Christian-Democratic People's Party (CVP), liberal Swiss Radical-Democratic Party (FDP), and Swiss Social-Democratic Party (SPS) and one from the Swiss People's Party (SVP) respectively. These seven form the Swiss Government.

Each year one of them is elected chairman with the title 'Federal President' but he has no real power. Each is head of one of seven departments. The Federal Council is run as a college, takes all decisions jointly and responsibility is shared.

The Federal Supreme Court is a completely independent body and its decisions cannot be influenced by Parliament or by the Government. Below the Federal Supreme Court are district and cantonal courts, many of which are run in a voluntary or semi-voluntary way.

Comments on Swiss Political Organisation

a. In that the two houses of Parliament are democratically elected, the Swiss people have control of the whole legislative body.

b. The fact that the second chamber, the States Council, represents the cantons gives the Swiss regions direct participation in law-making at the highest level.

c. In that the full cantons have two representatives and the half cantons one each, irrespective of the size of the canton or half canton, means that the smaller cantons in the States Council do not feel oppressed by the larger ones.

d. It is an advantage to have all Federal legislation debated and sanctioned by two independent political bodies in separate chambers.

e. Because the members of the Federal Council are drawn from four political parties, its members have the support of three-quarters of the members of Parliament. And also because the Federal Council acts as a college, with shared responsibility, it has been deemed the most stable government in the world. It is as a result of it being so stable that it is better able, if necessary, to pass unpopular laws.

f. The fact that the Government is so broadly based diminishes friction in Parliament and facilitates the legislative process.

g. In Switzerland there is no individual head of state. It is the only country in the world where a corporate body, in this case the Federal Council, acts as head of state, but ultimate political sovereignty rests with the people (the Sovereign).

THE SWISS PATTERN OF LEGISLATIVE PROCEDURE

Swiss Federal legislation is drafted and proposed to the Swiss Parliament by the Federal Council or Government.

The initiation for legislation usually comes from the Federal Council itself, but this body may have been promoted to draw up legislation by members of Parliament by means of a Motion or Postulate, from the cantons as the result of a Cantonal Initiative, or from the Swiss people themselves in the form of a Peoples' Initiative.

When the Federal Council has drawn up a draft measure it is submitted to the cantons and to a general hearing (Vernehmlassung) of all interested parties for their scrutiny and comment. This is then returned to the Federal Council. When satisfied as to its final form, the Federal Council will present the draft measure to Parliament.

It will then be decided which house shall debate it first, the National Council or the States Council. Having decided, that house will then appoint an inter-party committee to discuss the draft measure in detail and then present it to the chamber for plenary discussion. After this the measure will be handed on to the second chamber and the procedure repeated. Only after the measure has been accepted by both houses, in identical form, will it be returned to the Federal Council for ratification.

But the Swiss legislative procedure does not finish here, because all major acts of legislation in Switzerland must be approved also by the people and cantons, either directly by holding an Obligatory Referendum or tacitly, by default, in accordance with the Facultative Referendum option. If the measure would change the Federal Constitution in any way, or proposes entry into any international collective security organisation, or any supra-national society, it must be subjected to a referendum of both people and cantons. The Facultative or Optional Referendum applies to other Federal laws and decrees, where no amendment to the Federal Constitution is involved, or before the entering into of certain international treaties. After such a law has been passed, the Facultative Referendum leaves the cantons and enfranchized citizens free to demand a referendum on the measure within ninety days (minimum of 8 cantons or 50,000 enfranchized citizens).

The people and cantons also have the right to initiate legislation, providing they can obtain sufficient support for their proposal within eighteen months.

Characteristics of Swiss Legislative Procedure

Swiss legislative procedure promotes the political involvement of the Swiss people and cantons in the legislative process, in that both are allowed to initiate legislation by means of the People's and Cantonal Initiatives.

Political involvement of the people and cantons is also promoted by consulting both at the inception of legislation through the General Hearing (Vernehmlassung).

THE SWISS PATTERN OF POLITICAL REPRESENTATION

The aim of Swiss political representation is to promote and manifest as clear and as accurate an expression of the public will as possible.

To fulfil this aim, in elections to the various Swiss parliaments, both Federal and cantonal, two different voting-systems are used, namely the majority and the proportional representation voting methods.

The majority voting-system is usually employed if there are few candidates and if the emphasis is on the individual candidate; it is used in the election of the Federal Council, the States Council and most of the cantonal and commune governments. In the election of representatives to the National Council, however, it has been deemed fairer to employ principally the proportional representation method. In the election to the States Council where the majority system is used, at the first vote a candidate is usually required to obtain an absolute majority of votes cast to be elected. In subsequent votes, if these prove necessary, it is usually only required of a candidate that he or she need obtain the most voters cast to be elected.

The proportional representation voting-system was first introduced into Switzerland during the eighteen-nineties at cantonal level. The advantage of this system is that it gives greater opportunity for representation to the smaller parties. In this method of voting each political party compiles a list of candidates according to the number of seats available and these are submitted to the voter, together with a blank list. The voter has great freedom of choice. He can adopt the complete list of the party he favours, or if he disapproves of candidates on that list, he can delete their names and replace with names from other lists. If he especially approves of a candidate he can double-up, that is delete a name from the list and give his favoured candidate two votes. He can even compile his own list on the blank form, using the names of any of the valid candidates on any of the lists. Seats are then allocated to the various parties in proportion to the votes cast for them in each canton. If, as a result of an uneven number of votes cast an additional seat (Restmandat) remains unallocated, then this final allocation is made on the principle of the highest average of votes cast per seat, assuming that the final mandate were given to that party.

Comments on the Swiss Pattern of Political Representation

a. One advantage of the proportional representation voting-system is that no vote is lost; each vote counts, both to the candidate and to his or her party.

b. Where the proportional representation voting-system is employed the influence of the political parties is weakened, because the lists of candidates which they propose can be modified by the voter.

c. The fact that Swiss voters have a greater freedom of choice in the election of their political representatives gives them a more intense awareness of their political value.

THE SWISS PATTERN OF DIRECT DEMOCRACY

For the most part Switzerland is what is known as a semi-direct democracy, because twenty-one of her cantons are governed by parliaments elected by the people. The other five, however, Obwalden, Nidwalden, Appenzell-Ausserrhoden, Appenzell-Innerrhoden and Glarus, employ direct democracy in the administration of cantonal affairs, in that major cantonal political decisions are taken at public meetings by direct show-of-hands voting. These are called Landsgemeinde cantons.

They hold their annual public assembly (Landsgemeinde) either at the end of April or the beginning of May. These are very colourful occasions. Usually they are preceded by a church service after which the whole congregation processes to the assembly ground, led by a band and drummers to the accompaniment of the ringing of the church bells. The ancient banners are borne to the meeting place. The horn-blowers and the flag throwers accompany the sword and mace bearers together with the sergeants carrying the ancient sword and sceptre. All are clad in traditional costume.

The highest dignitary is the Landammann, who convenes the assembly and conducts its proceedings. His is an ancient office and it is highly respected. It includes both juridical and administrative competencies and, in addition, the Landammann is the official representative of the canton. These annual gatherings are taken very seriously by the people.

Direct democracy is also in evidence at commune level in the Commune Assembly which governs commune affairs. The Swiss citizens are deeply involved here, because in Switzerland the commune is responsible for carrying out tasks which, in other countries, would normally be the responsibility of a higher political authority. Most of this administrative work in the Swiss communes is carried out by ordinary Swiss citizens, for the most part in a voluntary or semi-voluntary capacity.

DISTINCTIVE FEATURES OF THE SWISS POLITICAL SYSTEM

A. SUBSIDIARITY

A distinctive characteristic of the Swiss democratic political system is that it is based upon the principle of 'subsidiarity', namely, that no task shall be deputed to a higher administrative authority which could be done equally well or better by a lesser, and that no task shall be performed by any authority which can be done equally well or better by the individual. As a result of compliance with this principle a maximum of tasks fall to the portion of the commune authorities. This is good because it is here, at commune level, that the citizen is most ready to participate in political and civic affairs.

In Switzerland the relative importance of the various tiers of political authority, national, cantonal and communal is often regarded inversely. In other words, the commune is regarded as being of most importance, the canton second and lastly the Federal State. This is because Switzerland, unlike other nations, has been developed from below upwards, not from above downwards. This inverted way of appraising the stratification of Swiss political organisation ensures that the people remain 'sovereign', and Switzerland democratic.

B. THE MILITIA-SYSTEM

Swiss political and social organisation is hallmarked by the 'militia-system', that is by a voluntary, or semi-voluntary, part-time participation of the Swiss people.

This is especially true of the Swiss political system, in which there are no professional, full-time members of parliament, either at national, cantonal or communal level. The Civil Defence services and Fire Service are also largely organised militia-wise. The Swiss Army is, for the most part, a militia-army, but here, as this is a compulsory duty for all Swiss males, wages and salaries are made up where necessary by social insurance. A vast amount of social work is done voluntarily by Swiss women in what is known as their 'Frauenverein' or Women's Organisation.

At commune level the bulk of civic administration is performed in a voluntary capacity by ordinary citizens. District courts and many cantonal courts are run militia-wise, as are numerous trade and professional organisations. Nor should the social work undertaken by members of the various churches be overlooked, nor that performed by members of political parties. All this voluntary work makes heavy demands on Swiss citizens, but as a result of it the cost of running the country is much reduced and therefore taxes can be kept to a minimum.

C. THE SOVEREIGNTY OF THE PEOPLE

In Switzerland the sovereignty of the people is largely ensured by the political rights which the Swiss people enjoy, and by the fact that the Swiss political system offers Swiss citizens the possibility of direct participation in political affairs. All Swiss parliaments, national, cantonal and communal are elected directly by the people. Every Swiss adult citizen has the right to vote and hold office, if elected, at all levels.

Swiss citizens have the right to propose legislation by means of the People's Initiative (providing they can obtain 100,000 valid signatures to the proposed measure within eighteen months). Eight cantons acting together have the same right.

The Swiss people also participate in the legislative process. First, they are offered the opportunity to comment on a proposed parliamentary measure, at an early stage, when it is offered for scrutiny to interested parties and the cantons, at a general hearing. Second, it is then piloted through the parliamentary process by their representatives and finally, the

Swiss people have the right to veto the measure by referendum before it can finally become law.

The Swiss people have an almost obsessive determination to ensure that the public will is given accurate and adequate political expression in the formulation of Swiss legislation. Hence their widespread use of the proportional representation voting-system, and the extensive opportunities, cited above, for the people to express their political views and assert their political authority.

D. THE CULT OF ACHIEVING CONSENSUS

The striving after friendly consensus in Switzerland has been called the overriding criterion of Swiss domestic political policy, and over the years sophisticated methods of negotiation have been devised in order to achieve it. The need for such consensus stems from ethnic, religious and political differences within the Swiss people. The Swiss population stems, largely, from four different peoples, three of which are from countries bordering on Switzerland and one indigenous group; four different languages are spoken by them. These differences were especially manifest in the First World War when half the Swiss population hoped for a German victory and the other half that of the Allies. There is also a very clear religious divide in Switzerland, in that half the population are Catholic and the other half Protestant. Politically there are differences of outlook also; the Swiss political spectrum stretches from extreme left to right of centre. In such a situation consensus had to be sought after, if any 'modus vivendi' were to be established in the country.

As a result of this quest for consensus in Swiss political affairs domestic harmony has been largely achieved in Switzerland, and thanks to that harmony, prosperity has come to the Swiss people. Political harmony was attained in 1957 when the Social Democrats abandoned their radical political outlook and this enabled them, from then on, to participate in government by electing two of their members to the Federal Council.

Industrial peace had already been achieved in 1937 with the signing of the Peace Agreement by both sides of the Metal and Watchmaking industry. They had decided that strikes and lock-outs were immature and in the end self-defeating. By signing this agreement they set a pattern of reconciliation for the whole of Swiss trade and industry. In consequence of this, there has been no major strike since that day and in 1986 not one day's work was lost in Switzerland through industrial strike action.

Social harmony came to Switzerland with the passing of humane and sensible social legislation by the Swiss Federal Parliament which alleviated the lot of the poorer people, and as prosperity increased and became more widespread after the Second World War.

E. THE CULT OF EQUITY

Equally as pronounced as their striving for political consensus is the Swiss search for equity among the Swiss people. This Swiss tradition of 'fairness' stretches back at least as far as the incursion of the Alemanni into present-day Switzerland. The Alemanni firmly believed in the owning of private property, but in deference to the poorer members of their communities they always reserved a portion of the land surrounding their villages as common land, to be jointly owned and administered, and also a place where everyone could graze their animals.

Today fairness in Switzerland is exemplified by the fact that all Swiss citizens are equal before the Law and in status, and all Swiss adults have equal political and civil rights. In Swiss state schools, primary, secondary, vocational and further education are free to all children, and as around ninety-five per cent of all Swiss children attend these schools there is a large degree of equality of opportunity. In the Swiss Army all recruits start at the same level and promotion is based on character and ability. Swiss taxation is based on ability to pay, and in the division of funds between the Federal State, the cantons and the communes a system of compensation for the poorer party ensures an equitable distribution. Switzerland is very largely a classless society with no social titles or distinctions save that of 'Alt Bundesrat' for retired Federal Councillors.

POLITICAL ATTRIBUTES OF THE SWISS PEOPLE

The effective functioning of a political system is, however, ultimately dependent on the efficiency of its operators. As in Switzerland many political and social functions are carried out militia-wise (that is on a voluntary or semi-voluntary basis) it means that the effectiveness of the system is largely dependent on the competence of the people themselves and, above all, upon their political maturity. What, then, makes for political maturity in Switzerland?

First, a sign of maturity, on the part of the individual citizen, is a readiness to compromise with one's fellows. The Swiss had the great good fortune to suffer a humiliating military defeat at the Battle of Marignano in 1515 at the hands of French and Papal forces. They withdrew within their own territories and from then on adopted a policy of non-aggressive neutrality. Non-belligerent attitudes gradually became a part of Swiss make-up, so that for many Swiss, to come to terms with one's adversary became the highest good.

Second, the fact that for centuries the Swiss were desperately poor meant that they had to fend for themselves. This inculcated a sense of civic responsibility and a willingness to co-operate with their fellows. This fellow-feeling is evidenced today in Switzerland by the readiness of the Swiss people to pay higher prices for farm produce in order to subsidize the mountain farmers. The Swiss quickly learned that every entitlement brings with it an obligation. A Swiss male still gives a year of his life to his country in military service; in addition he does fire-service and civil-defence duties in his spare time, either voluntarily or semi-voluntarily.

Third, further evidence of the political maturity of the Swiss people is that they are able to forgo immediate gratification for future benefit. This was made apparent in their approach to the creation of an Old Age and Bereavement Insurance scheme. As early as 1925 it was decided that provision should be made in the Federal Constitution for the introduction of such a scheme, and also that, in typical Swiss fashion, it should be jointly financed by the Federal State, the cantons, the employers and the employees. The question arose as to how the Federal State could provide part of its share. Either it could borrow the money, which would have to be paid back later, or the scheme could be deferred until such time as the required funds had been saved and invested, so as to yield sufficient interest to make good the contributions required of the Federal State. The Swiss people decided upon the more responsible course of deferring the introduction of the scheme until such time as the necessary funds had been saved and invested. In order to do this the Federal tax on tobacco was specifically earmarked for the purpose of financing the scheme and placed in a special fund. The fund grew so rapidly that in 1947 the interest from the investments was deemed sufficient to complete the contribution required of the Federal State and the scheme was introduced. By adopting this policy of saving first, no additional financial burden was placed upon the next generation.

In that the Swiss people are the final arbiters in Swiss political affairs, it is essential that they should be well informed on current topics which they may have to vote upon. When the Federal Parliament is in session a part of the evening television news gives coverage to the day's debate with excerpts given of each point of view. For a Swiss population of around six and a half million almost three and a half million newspapers are printed daily and it is estimated that between eighty and ninety per cent of Swiss male youth read a serious newspaper each day.

In any assessment of the development of Swiss political thinking and structures the influence exercised by Christian teaching on the Swiss people throughout the ages should not be minimised. Switzerland was first influenced by Christianity through travellers and soldiers from Rome early in the Christian era, but a widespread conversion of the people did not occur until the sixth century and this was prompted by

Irish monks from the monastery of Luxeuil in France. Later Swiss religious thinkers played a prominent part in the Reformation, especially Zwingli in Zürich and Calvin in Geneva, and their teachings had a profound effect on Swiss political thought and outlook.

In the late nineteen century certain trade unions were founded by Swiss churches and this is thought to have been one of the reasons why Swiss trade unionism has never been as radical as in other countries and consequently less disruptive of trade and industry.

The effect of Christian teaching is also reflected in the aims of Swiss political parties founded under the aegis of both major Swiss religious confessions, namely Roman Catholicism and Protestantism. The Swiss Christian-Democratic People's Party (CVP), which originally was predominantly a Roman Catholic party, states categorically in its manifesto that the Swiss Christian-Democratic People's Party ideologically affirms its commitment to Christianity. The Evangelical People's Party (EVP) manifesto states that the Evangelical People's Party is a group of people who accept that political responsibility stems from the Christian Gospel and wish to put it into practice at commune, cantonal and Federal level, and in worldwide affairs.

Perhaps the degree of responsibility, and thereby the political maturity, evidenced by the Swiss people is best exemplified by the oath taken each year at the Appenzell-Ausserrhoden Landsgemeinde, namely 'to promote the well-being and honour of the Fatherland and protect it from harm, to administer the cantonal constitution and laws, to protect, safeguard and procure justice for widows, orphans and everyone to the best of one's ability as law and conscience direct, and not to be prevailed upon through friendship or feud, or for any other reason, to be diverted from so doing'.

It is this maturity of outlook on the part of the Swiss citizens and the degree of development of Swiss political organisation which makes of Switzerland a political federation worthy of consideration by the outside world.